Master Chefs for Home Chefs / 04

52 world-class recipes

Foreword

Dear Reader,

This is a book filled with recipes from all over the world, carefully created by the earth's great chefs for those who love food to replicate at home. But there is one very special recipe that you won't find in this cookbook. It's a truly global recipe - the World Food Programme uses a version of it in thousands of schools in more than 70 countries. It's a recipe for a simple basic school lunch.

You boil some rice - or whatever grain or cereal is preferred locally - preferably on a fuel-efficient stove to save firewood and protect the environment. Separately you cook some beans, lentils or split peas for protein, seasoned with oil and salt. If your students have been able to get any vegetables - perhaps from the school garden they cultivate, or perhaps from their parents - then you could add those for extra flavour. It's not complicated to cook, but you'd better make sure it's ready in time for lunch, when the students will be lining up to receive their cup full of food - the one meal they know for sure they're going to get that day.

This is the essence of WFP's school meal programme, providing children with a simple meal and encouraging them to come to school so that they can have hope for a better future. The proceeds from this cookbook will ensure that 40 students, who have no other food, will not go to school hungry. Thank you for supporting WFP's school meal programme, and happy cooking!

Josette Sheeran

Executive Director
United Nations World Food Programme

What does WFP do?

The United Nations World Food Programme (WFP) is the world's largest humanitarian organisation fighting hunger worldwide. Every year, WFP feeds an average of 90 million people in more than 70 countries.

One of WFP's projects is the school meals programme, which provides a free school lunch or snack to poor children in school. The concept is simple: food attracts hungry children to school, and they get an education that can help them break out of the cycle of hunger and poverty. This is especially important for girls, who are the first to be kept at home in poor families. For many parents, these meals are a reason for sending their children to school rather than out to work. It only costs WFP 20 Euro cents to provide a child with a nourishing meal at school.

Hunger is the greatest threat to health worldwide. It claims more lives each year than AIDS, malaria and tuberculosis combined. Over one billion people in the world are undernourished, most of them women and children. A third of all child deaths in the developing world are linked to undernutrition.

WFP

wfp.org

For more information about WFP
visit www.wfp.org.

Content

Starters/Recipe no 1 - 22

Page 9

Main Courses/Recipe no 23 - 42

Page 55

Desserts/Recipe no 43 - 52

Page 97

Chef Index

Page 118

Starters

01/ Pumpkin, Cucumber and
Horseradish Salad
Jonnie Boer/De Librije

02/ Tempura-Fried King Prawns
with Squid Ink and Zucchini and Mussel Sauce
Moreno Cedroni/Madonnina del Pescatore

03/ Beetroot Tart with Goat's Cheese Mousse
Luke Dale-Roberts/La Colombe

04/ Wrap with Smoked Salmon,
Pickled Ginger and Pesto
Edwin Kats/InterContinental Nanjing

05/ Poached Egg in Romaine Lettuce
Pierre Gagnaire/Pierre Gagnaire

06/ Grilled Anchovies and Artichokes
with Wild Rocket Leaves
Victor Arguinzoniz/Asador Etxebarri

07/ Salad with Wild Herbs, Steak Tartar,
Banyuls Vinegar and Walnut Oil
Sven Elverfeld/Aqua

08/ Fried King Prawns with Avocado
and Watermelon Salad and
Coriander Mayonnaise
Jean Beddington/Restaurant Beddington's

09/ Mixed Bean Salad with Zucchini, Cherries
and Pistachio Vinaigrette
Mauro Colagreco/Mirazur

10/ Rooibos Bisque with Lobster
and Poached Egg
Ramon Beuk/Ramon Beuk

11/ Salicornia Risotto with Capers and Coffee
Sergio Herman/Oud Sluis

12/ Steamed Haddock with Russian Potato
Salad, Hand-Peeled Grey Prawns, Salicornia,
Herring Roe and Beurre Noisette
Gert-Jan Cieremans/Seinpost

13/ Rigatoni Volcanoes
Alfonso Iaccarino/Don Alfonso 1890

14/ Grilled Monkfish with Cream of Green Peas,
Walnut Salsa and Pomegranate Seeds
Jon-Filip Johannessen/Mathuset Solvold

15/ Zuppa alla Pavese with Quail
and Curried Cherries
Davide Oldani/D'O

16/ Marinated Barbecued King Prawns
Neil Perry/Rockpool

17/ Beetroot Soup with Poached
Quail Eggs
Mirko Reeh/Restaurant Pearl by Mirko Reeh

18/ Lukewarm Artichoke Salad with Herbs
Heinz Reitbauer/Steirereck Stadtpark

19/ Marinated Salmon with
Tamago and Spinach
Emmanuel Stroobant/Restaurant Saint Pierre

20/ Tender Lobster with Melon
Salad and Ham Mousse
Erik van Loo/Restaurant Parkheuvel

21/ Citrus pesto
Filippo La Mantia/Filippo la Mantia

22/ Carpaccio of Scallops with Porcini
Mushrooms, Granny Smith Apples and
Aceto di Vin Santo
Phillipe Rochat/Restaurant de l'Hotel de Ville

Pumpkin, Cucumber and Horseradish Salad

Jonnie Boer/De Librije

Preparation

1/ Add vinegar and sugar to 3/4 cup of water and bring to a boil. Allow to boil for a short while, then remove pan from heat. Add bay leaf, red pepper and pepper corns and allow to cool.

2/ Cut a piece of pumpkin into a chunk of 1" x 6". Slice ribbons from it using a vegetable peeler, then soak these in the sugar-and-vinegar mixture. Cut 3/4 of the pumpkin into pieces and cook with one clove of garlic, orange juice, salt and rosemary for 20 min. until done. Purée until completely smooth and season with salt and pepper. Allow to cool, then pour the mixture into a piping bag.

3/ Remove pumpkin ribbons from the sugar-and-vinegar mixture and arrange two ribbons like a plus symbol. Pat dry and squirt enough pumpkin purée in the centre to create a 'cushion'.

4/ Cut the remaining pumpkin into cubes and lay them in the sugar-and-vinegar mixture. Peel 1 cucumber, remove the seeds, cut into small cubes and place in the sugar-and-vinegar mixture.

5/ Gently heat the milk and stir the goat's cheese through it until smooth and mix with the drained pieces of cucumber. Scoop the mixture into a piping bag and place in refrigerator.

6/ Peel 1 cucumber lengthwise as thin as possible without reaching the seeds at the centre. Stack all the strips, cut the pile into 3 equal pieces and then in half. Place the cucumber strips on cling film in an overlapping pattern. Fold the cling film double and turn the bundle around. Carefully peel back the cling film and squirt the cheese mixture evenly in the centre. Roll up the strips so that they form a cylinder shape. Remove the cling film. Carefully slice the cylinder into 4 pieces. Make two cylinders.

7/ Squeeze 1 cucumber, add the shallot and garlic, and leave it for at least 1 hour. Sieve the mixture and season with vinegar, salt and pepper.

8/ Mix the yogurt, crème fraîche, horseradish sauce, mustard and salt to taste; transfer to a piping bag and chill in refrigerator until firm.

9/ Lay the cucumber rolls and pumpkin bundles in a deep plate; arrange the pumpkin cubes, carrot, purslane and corn salad around it. Squirt several dots of the horseradish yogurt. Pour the juice over the dish at the table.

Ingredients 4p

1 cup sugar
12.5 tbsp vinegar
1 tsp black pepper corns
1 small red pepper, halved
1 bay leaf
1 pumpkin, peeled
2 cloves of garlic, peeled
The juice of one orange
1 sprig of rosemary
3 cucumbers
1/3 lb of Sainte-Maure (soft) goat's cheese
4 tsp milk
1/2 shallot
1/2 cup yogurt
1/2 cup crème fraîche
1 tbsp horseradish sauce
1 tsp whole-grain mustard
3 tbsp sushi vinegar
1 carrot, flash-cooked and chopped
a handful of corn salad leaves
a handful of purslane

Requirements
Piping bag and juice extractor

Wine suggestion
Jurançon sec 2006, Henri Lapouble Laplace, France

Under the inspired direction of chef Jonnie Boer, De Librije in the Dutch town of Zwolle has earned three Michelin stars. This accomplishment has made Boer and his wife Thérèse national celebrities in the Netherlands, where they have also become the stars of a popular reality show.

Tempura-Fried King Prawns with Squid Ink and Zucchini and Mussel Sauce

Moreno Cedroni/Madonnina del Pescatore

Preparation

1/ Heat the oil in a large pan and stir in the finely chopped garlic. Add the mussels. Turn the heat up high, add the wine, let it reduce somewhat and then add the zucchini slices to the pan. Cover pan and cook until the mussels open. Remove pan from heat and remove mussels from shells.

2/ Add 1/2 cup of water to the squid ink. Mix the flour and the yeast with the diluted squid ink, along with a pinch of salt and a pinch of sugar. Let the batter rise for 30 minutes.

3/ Heat the oil in a pan approximately 8" in diameter until it reaches 355°F (use a thermometer). Drag the prawns through the batter and deep-fry them. Let them drain and season with a little salt.

4/ Spoon 2 spoonfuls of zucchini and mussel sauce onto a plate. Add a drop of lemon juice. Arrange the prawns and slices of daikon radish in the middle of the plate.

Ingredients 4p

5 tbsp extra virgin olive oil
1/2 clove of garlic
2 lb 3 oz cleaned mussels
1 1/4 tbsp dry white wine
2 zucchinis
1 tbsp squid ink (from fishmonger)
10 tbsp flour
0,5 oz fresh yeast (from bakery)
(Alternatively, 2.5 tsp dry yeast)
1 tsp sugar
8 cups olive oil for deep frying
11 oz peeled king prawns
Lemon juice
2 oz daikon radish (alternatively, regular radish), cut into small pieces

Requirements
Thermometer

Wine suggestion
Velenosi brut Metodo Classico

Moreno Cedroni is the Michelin two-star chef and co-owner, with his wife Mariella, of the restaurant La Madonnina del Pescatore, which they opened in 1984 in Senigallia, on the Adriatic coast in the Marche region.

Beetroot Tart with Goat's Cheese Mousse

Luke Dale-Roberts/La Colombe

Preparation

1/ Preheat oven to 320°F.

2/ Line the moulds with cling film.

3/ Purée the goat's cheese in the food processor or with the hand blender.

4/ Soften the gelatine in water, heat the white wine and bring to a boil, then remove from heat. Stir in the gelatine and, with the food processor running, add the mixture to the goat's cheese.

5/ Carefully blend the mixture with the whipped cream, spoon into the moulds and allow to firm in the refrigerator.

6/ Take 2 beetroots and chop them very finely, mix with the sugar, oil and season with salt and pepper, then slice the other 2 beetroots into very thin slices.

7/ Place the puff pastry squares on a greased baking tray. Spoon some of the beetroot mixture in the middle of each square, then arrange slices of beetroot around them like a flower, season with salt and brush the edges of the pastry with egg yolk.

8/ Bake the beetroot tarts in the middle of the oven for 15 minutes until done.

9/ Remove the goat's cheese mousse from the moulds. On each plate, place a warm beetroot tart and lay a goat's cheese mousse on top of it, allowing it to melt slightly. Garnish with some capers, olive oil and balsamic vinegar.

Ingredients 10 tarts

1.5 tsp of gelatine
2/3 cup white wine
1/3 lb soft goat's cheese
1 1/4 cups whipped cream
4 cooked beetroots, peeled
1 tsp sugar
1 tbsp olive oil
10 squares of puff pastry, defrosted
2 egg yolks, lightly beaten
1 tbsp capers
1 tbsp extra virgin olive oil
1 tbsp balsamic vinegar

Requirements

12 moulds the size of an egg cup
Cling film
Food processor or hand blender

Wine suggestion

Soave Monte Fiorentine 2008,
Ca'Rugate, Veneto, Italy

The celebrated La Colombe in Cape Town serves a creative blend of French and Asian cuisine, which is credited to the arrival of chef Luke Dale-Roberts in 2006. He adds Eastern influences to the classic and contemporary French cuisine for which La Colombe has received many awards both in South Africa and internationally. Dale-Roberts and his restaurant have been named South African Chef of the Year (2008) and Restaurant of the Year (2009) respectively.

Wrap with Smoked Salmon, Pickled Ginger and Pesto

Edwin Kats/InterContinental Nanjing

Preparation

1/ Cut the carrot, celery root and potato into very thin slices. Halve the leek and cut into pieces.

2/ Heat the oil in the deep frying pan to 355°F and fry the vegetables in batches until crunchy. Allow to drain on a paper towel and sprinkle with salt.

3/ Mix the pesto and the crème fraiche and spread on the wraps, then divide the salmon and ginger on top. Roll the wrap tightly, wrap in cling film and place in the refrigerator for at least 1 hour.

4/ Cut the wraps into slices. Place as much mixed salad as you desire on a plate with some wrap slices on top, then garnish with the fried vegetable chips.

Ingredients 4p

1 carrot
1/4 celery root (celeriac)
1 potato
1 leek
A few leaves of fresh spinach
3 tbsp basil pesto
4 tbsp crème fraiche
4 wraps
9 oz thinly sliced smoked salmon
4 tbsp pickled ginger
Mixed salad

Requirements

Deep frying pan with oil

Wine suggestion

Furmint 2007, Dobogó,
Tokaj, Ungarn

Edwin Kats, the former star chef of La Rive, the restaurant at the Amstel Hotel,
is now making a name for himself in China.

Poached Egg in Romaine Lettuce

Pierre Gagnaire/Pierre Gagnaire

Preparation

1/ Preheat oven to 440°F. Form foil into 4 boat-shaped trays and coat them with butter. Cover the bottom of a dish with coarse salt and place the trays inside.

2/ Crack an egg into each of the trays, cover with tin foil and bake in the oven for 10 minutes.

3/ Cut the eggplant into cubes and sauté in 2 tbsps of oil until golden brown.

4/ Cut 4 mushrooms into thin slices, set aside to use as garnish later, and cut the remaining mushrooms into small pieces.

5/ Sauté the mushroom pieces in 2 tbsps of oil and mash them into small pieces. Add the eggplant, crème fraîche, cottage cheese and ginger. Bring to a boil; then remove pan from the heat immediately. Finally, add chives, parsley and culatello.

6/ Divide the vegetable mixture between the four plates. Place a poached egg in a leaf of Romaine lettuce and lay it on top. Season with chervil, salt and pepper and a few drops of balsamic vinegar. Lay on the plate and add the remaining mushroom slices.

Ingredients 4p

1 firm eggplant
4-5 tbsp grape seed oil
2 cups white mushrooms
a small knob unpeeld fresh ginger, cubed
1 cup cottage cheese
1 tbsp semi-skimmed crème fraîche
4 tbsp chives and parsley, chopped
2 oz culatello or prosciutto, in thick strips
4 eggs
2 tbsp butter
4 leaves Romaine lettuce
A few sprigs of chervil
1 tbsp white balsamic vinegar

Requirements

Tin foil
1 lb coarse salt

Wine suggestion

Meursault 'Limozin',
Henri Germain 2007, Germany.

One of a select group of three-Michelin-starred chefs, Pierre Gagnaire was one of the pioneers of the fusion style, creating often bizarre blends of flavours, aromas, textures and ingredients. He is currently the owner and chef at Sketch in London, Twist in Las Vegas, and Pierre Gagnaire in Paris, all three of which have been ranked among the world's finest restaurants by the international food press.

Grilled Anchovies and Artichokes with Wild Rocket Leaves

Victor Arguinzoniz/Asador Etxebarri

Preparation

1/ Remove the heads of the anchovies, cut the stomachs completely open and lay them open. Place two opened anchovies on top of each other with the skin of each on the outside. Sprinkle with oil.

2/ Heat up the grill or grill pan. Cut each artichoke into quarters, sprinkle with oil and grill for 2-3 minutes, turning over halfway through.

3/ Mix the remaining oil with the grated lemon peel and juice, season with sea salt and spoon the lemon oil over the rocket.

4/ Grill the anchovies on a medium flame, season with salt and Txakoli, turn over and grill for another 2 minutes. Season the anchovies with salt and Txakoli and serve with the artichokes and rocket salad.

Ingredients 4p

8 fresh anchovies, cleaned
4 baby artichokes, cooked
4 oz wild rocket leaves, washed
1/2 lemon, grated and squeezed
1/2 cup good-quality olive oil
3 tbsp Txakoli or
dry white wine

Requirements

Grill or grill pan

Wine suggestion

Fiano di Avelino 2009, Feudi di San Gregorio, Kampanien, Italy

Grill wizard Victor Arguinzoniz, a native of Spain, can grill everything you can imagine (even caviar), creating a revolutionary new cuisine in the process.

Salad with Wild Herbs, Steak Tartar, Banyuls Vinegar and Walnut Oil

Sven Elverfeld/Aqua

Preparation

1/ Cut the meat into very small cubes and blend with one shallot, the capers, anchovies, mustard and grape seed oil. Season with salt and pepper.

2/ Wash the wild herbs in cold water and dry them carefully (in a salad spinner). Break into the desired size. You should use only the petals from the large flowers. Cover and store in a cool place.

3/ Whisk the rest of the shallot with the chicken stock, Banyuls vinegar and walnut oil into a dressing and season with sugar, salt and pepper.

4/ Mix the wild herbs and chives with the vinaigrette.

5/ Divide the steak tartar between four plates with the help of a circular mould and spoon the salad on top. Garnish the plate with a few drops of walnut oil and herb pesto around the steak tartar.

6/ In addition, if desired, you can cut up small cubes of walnut bread and bake them in a little walnut oil until golden brown. Serve them on top of the salad.

Ingredients 4p

12 oz beef sirloin or beef tenderloin (or very fresh tartar)
2 shallots, finely chopped
1 tbsp capers, finely chopped
1 tbsp anchovies, finely chopped
1 tsp Dijon mustard
1 tbsp grape seed oil
Seasonal wild herbs and flowers, such as galinsoga, elder, bronze fennel, oxalis, yarrow, etc.
1 tbsp Banyuls vinegar (or a very good-quality balsamic vinegar)
4-5 tbsp walnut oil
2 tbsp condensed chicken stock
1 dash of sugar
2 tbsp finely chopped chives

Requirements
3-4" in circular mould

Wine suggestion
2009 Sauvignon Blanc
from the Klein Constantia Estate
South Africa

Aqua, which has been awarded three Michelin stars, has thrived for ten years under the leadership of Sven Elverfeld, who is currently ranked among Germany's culinary elite. His tendency to draw inspiration from the industrial world of Autostadt in Wolfsburg makes his dishes all the more fascinating. Elverfeld's cuisine has garnered praise from all over the world, with Gault Millau awarding him 19 points and the trade magazine Der Feinschmecker a 5F.

Fried King Prawns with Avocado and Watermelon Salad and Coriander Mayonnaise

Jean Beddington/Restaurant Beddington's

Preparation

1/ Peel the tomatoes and the cucumber. Cut the tomatoes, cucumber, avocado and watermelon into cubes of 0.5". Finely chop the coriander and grate and squeeze the lime.

2/ Make a dressing of 2 1/2 tbsp of olive oil and the two types of vinegar, and add salt and pepper to taste.

3/ Mix the tomato, cucumber, avocado and watermelon. Combine with the dressing.

4/ Purée the coriander, lime juice and mayonnaise with a hand blender. In a hot non-stick frying pan, fry the king prawns in a little oil until golden brown and sprinkle them with a little coarse sea salt.

5/ Add a strip of mayonnaise across the plate and add one quarter of the salad on top using a ring-shaped mould. Arrange 3 king prawns on the plate and garnish with some grated lime peel and fresh herbs.

Ingredients 4p

3 beefsteak tomatoes
1 cucumber
1 avocado
1/4 watermelon, seeded
3 tbsp extra virgin olive oil
1 tbsp white wine vinegar
1 tbsp balsamic vinegar
1/4 bunch of fresh coriander, finely chopped
1/2 lime, grated and squeezed
3 tbsp mayonnaise
12 king prawns, peeled and heads removed
coarse sea salt
Fresh herbs to taste

Requirements

Hand blender, ring-shaped mould

Wine suggestion

Pinot Blanc 'Kritt' 2008, Marc Kreijdenweiss, Elzas, France

Jean Beddington learned to cook from her mother and grandmother as a young girl. After a world trip she ended up in Japan, where she was trained in traditional Japanese shizen shoku (natural food) cuisine. She opened her Amsterdam restaurant, Beddington's, in 1983.

Mixed Bean Salad with Zucchini, Cherries and Pistachio Vinaigrette

Mauro Colagreco/Mirazur

Preparation

1/ Chop the pistachios into small pieces and roast them in a dry frying pan. Allow to cool.

2/ Make a vinaigrette of olive oil, vinegar, pistachios and chopped shallot. Add salt and pepper to taste.

3/ Cook all the beans separately in water until tender, adding salt, then cool them in ice water. Drain and pat dry.

4/ Use a vegetable slicer to slice the zucchini into long ribbons.

5/ Season the beans with ginger, the remaining oil, and sea salt. Serve the beans on a flat plate. Pile them up high, then add the zucchini ribbons, cherries and rocket leaves. Finally, add the pistachio vinaigrette.

Ingredients 4p

1/2 cup roasted pistachios
4-5 tbsp olive oil
2 tsp white balsamic vinegar or sherry vinegar
1 shallot
2 cups runner beans
1 cup lima beans
1 cup green beans
1 zucchini
1 piece of ginger root, grated
Rocket leaves
Sea salt
1/2 cup red and white cherries, pits removed

Requirements

Grill or Grill pan

Wine suggestion

Saint Joseph Domaine Montez white 'Duc de Monteillet'

Argentine-born chef Mauro Colagreco is firmly in touch with his Italian and Spanish roots, as he demonstrates to perfection at his restaurant Mirazur, located in the orchards of Menton on the French Riviera. Mirazur received a Michelin star within a year of its opening, and Colagreco is the first non-French chef to have been awarded the title of Chef of the Year by the Gault Millau Guide.

Rooibos Bisque with Lobster and Poached Egg

Ramon Beuk/Ramon Beuk

Preparation

1/ Bring a large pot of water to a boil. Cook the lobsters for 4 minutes, remove from pan and allow to cool. Twist off the lobster tails, cut them lengthwise and remove the meat. Rinse the breasts under the tap and cut into pieces. Break the claws and carefully remove the meat. Separate the shells and claws to use for the bisque.

2/ Heat 4 tbsp of oil in a pan and fry the lobster shells and claws. Quarter the (unpeeled) shallots and add them along with the unpeeled garlic. Add the tomato purée and the wine. Add the tea bags and enough water to cover the lobster shells; then bring to a boil. Turn down the heat and allow to sit for 1 hour.

3/ Strain the solid ingredients through a sieve and reduce liquid until 1 cup remain. Season with salt and pepper.

4/ Just before serving, add the butter and whisk the bisque with the hand blender.

5/ Mix 2 cups of water with the vinegar in a pan and bring to a boil. Turn down the heat and carefully crack the ice-cold eggs just above the water. Cook for 6 minutes until done. Remove from pan and place in a large amount of cold water.

6/ On each plate, arrange one egg and a piece of lobster beside it. Spoon the bisque around it and garnish with the basil leaves. Cut the egg open just before serving.

Ingredients 4p

Two lobsters (1 lb each)
4 tbsp oil
2 shallots
3 cloves of garlic
2 tbsp tomato purée
1 cup white wine
4 Rooibos tea bags
3 1/2 tbsp butter
4 ice-cold, fresh eggs
1/2 cup vinegar
Baby basil leaves for garnish

Requirements

Hand blender

Wine suggestion

Canaiuolo Rosé 2009,
Montenidoli, Toskana, Italy

Ramon Beuk is a well know chef in the Netherlands for presenting TV-shows, his columns and books he's written. Besides that he is an entrepreneur with a creative spirit. Successful companies of Ramon Beuk are his event company, CuliPro and live catering Food Emotions.

Salicornia Risotto with Capers and Coffee

Sergio Herman/Oud Sluis

Preparation

1/ Shred the shallot and finely chop the garlic.

2/ Sauté the shallot and garlic in 1 tbsp of oil, add the rice and stew gently, adding the white wine. When the wine has evaporated, add half of the stock to the rice. Let the stock evaporate and then add more. Repeat this process until the rice is almost done.

3/ Grate the Parmesan and add it to the rice mixture along with the butter and cream. Cover and, after 10 minutes, carefully stir the mixture into a creamy risotto. Mix the raw salicornia (reserving a few tips) and the capers through the risotto.

4/ Season with lime juice. Sprinkle the salicornia tips with the remaining oil and add them to the risotto. Sprinkle coffee over the dish to taste.

Ingredients 2p

2 tbsp olive oil
2 shallots
1 clove of garlic
3/4 cup risotto rice
1 tbsp white wine
2 cups chicken stock
1 oz Parmesan cheese
1 tbsp salted butter
1/4 cup cream
6 tbsp capers, drained
7 oz salicornia
The juice of 1 lime
1-2 tbsp ground coffee

Wine suggestion
Blanc de Blancs 2008, Domaine Ott, Provence, France

Sergio Herman, the chef at the three-Michelin-starred restaurant Oud Sluis in the Dutch Province of Zeeland, is an important representative of a new generation of European chefs. His particular brand of culinary magic is all about professional knowledge, the latest cooking techniques, a dash of flair and the very best ingredients that his native Zeeland has to offer.

Steamed Haddock with Russian Potato Salad, Hand-Peeled Grey Shrimps, Salicornia, Herring Roe and Beurre Noisette

Gert-Jan Cieremans/Seinpost

Preparation

1/ Boil the celeriac and potatoes, stew the onion until tender and peel the apple. Cut the celeriac, onion, apple, potato and dill pickles into tiny cubes and chop the parsley finely. Mix everything together.

2/ Make a dressing with the stock, oil, vinegar, mustard and dill pickles juice, season with salt and pepper and spoon through the vegetable mixture. This is the Russian potato salad.

3/ Cut the salicornia into 0.6" pieces and sauté in olive oil.

4/ Steam the haddock on a rack over boiling water (covering the pan) for 7-9 minutes until done.

5/ Mix the melted butter with the prawns and mix the beurre noisette with the herring roe. Divide the fish among four plates, then add the prawns and Russian potato salad.

6/ Garnish the dish with the herring roe and salicornia.

Makes for an elegant, light spring lunch, with the fresh and salty flavours enhancing the fish.

Ingredients 4p

1.4 oz boiled celeriac
1 onion stewed until tender
1 sour apple (e.g. Granny Smith)
2 boiled potatoes
4 dill pickles, seeded
1/2 bunch of leaf parsley
8 tbsp chicken stock
8 tbsp olive oil
4 tbsp wine vinegar
4 tbsp Dijon mustard
4 tsp dill pickle juice (from jar)
4 thick haddock fillets
4 tbsp melted warm butter
3.5 oz grey shrimps
4 tbsp beurre noisette
(heat the butter in the pan until it turns nutty brown)
4 tsp herring roe
4 tbsp salicornia

Wine suggestion
The fresh, saline Picpoul de Pinet
(Languedoc)

Gert-Jan Cieremans is the owner of Seinpost in the Dutch seaside resort of Scheveningen.
The restaurant has earned 15 Gault Millau points and a Michelin star.

Rigatoni Volcanoes

Alfonso Iaccarino/Don Alfonso 1890

Preparation

1/ Soak the breadcrumbs in 1 tbsp of milk, then drain; mix with 1 egg and the ground meat. Season with salt and pepper and shape into small balls. Boil the other egg for 7 minutes and slice into pieces.

2/ Dip half of the basil into boiling water and then immediately into ice water. Stir 1 tbsp of oil through the leaves; then strain mixture through a fine chinois (cone-shaped sieve).

3/ Heat 3 tbsps of milk and one quarter of the mozzarella in a bowl suspended above a pan of boiling water; when the cheese has melted, stir through a fine, cone-shaped sieve. Cut the remaining mozzarella into pieces. Mix the onion with the peas. Cook the rigatoni for 3 minutes and mix with the tomato sauce and basil.

4/ Preheat oven to 320°F. Place some mozzarella on the bottom of each ramekin. Fill the sides with pasta, and in the middle place the peas, meatballs, boiled egg and basil. Cover with the mozzarella. Place the ramekins in the middle of the oven for 15 minutes.

4/ Place a plate on top of the ramekins and turn them upside down, allowing the contents to come out. Garnish with the mozzarella sauce, balsamic vinegar, the remaining basil and oil to taste.

Ingredients 4p

1/4 cup breadcrumbs
4 tbsp milk
3.5 oz mixed ground beef and pork
2 eggs
1 bunch of fresh basil
4 tbsp extra virgin olive oil
1/2 small onion, sautéd
1/3 cup peas
3 cups rigatoni pasta
1 buffalo mozzarella
1 cup tomato sauce
4 tbsp balsamic vinegar

Requirements

Chinois (a cone-shaped sieve)
4 ramekins of approx. 3"
diameter, greased

Wine suggestion

Regaleali Bianco 2009, Tasca d'Almerita, Sizilien, Italy

In their sun-kissed garden on the island of Capri, Alfonso and Livia Iaccarino grow their own herbs, lemons, peaches, artichokes, zucchinis, tomatoes and olives. Their sought-after restaurant Don Alfonso is located in Sorrento, on the mainland off Capri.

Grilled Monkfish with Cream of Green Peas, Walnut Salsa and Pomegranate Seeds

Jon-Filip Johannessen/Mathuset Solvold

Preparation

1/ Set one pat of butter aside, then melt the rest, let it stand briefly and clarify by spooning off the foam that forms.

2/ Cook the peas for 5 minutes and remove from the water. Purée the peas in the blender with 30 grams of butter; season with salt.

3/ Heat up a frying pan. Sear the fish briskly on both sides at a high heat, then add the reserved pat of butter and cook for 8 minutes. Season with grated lemon peel, salt and pepper.

4/ Mix the still-warm clarified butter with the walnut and season with lemon juice, salt and pepper.

5/ Serve the fish with the cream of green peas and the walnut salsa. Garnish with pomegranate seeds.

Ingredients 4p

7 tbsp butter

2 1/4 cups green peas

14 oz monkfish, at room temperature and cut into 4 pieces

1 lemon, grated

3 tbsp shelled walnuts, cut into pieces

1 tbsp pomegranate seeds

Wine suggestion

Vernaccia di San Gimignano 2008, Montenidoli, Toskana, Italy

As one of the best restaurants in Norway, Solvold is a wonderful place for a party. The interior design is tasteful, modern and inspired by Scandinavian design trends.

Zuppa alla Pavese with Quail and Curried Cherries

Davide Oldani/D'O

Preparation

1/ Heat the oil in a soup pan and sauté the vegetables in the oil. Add the quail bones and chicken stock. Bring to a boil and skim off the foam. Turn down the heat and allow to simmer for 3 hours. Strain the soup through a strainer and keep warm.

2/ Sprinkle the quails with salt, heat the oil and sauté the quails in it. Remove from the heat and keep warm.

3/ Bring the water to a boil in a pan and add the vinegar. Reduce the heat. With a spoon, stir the water to create a 'funnel'. Crack the quail eggs and add them to the water one by one. Poach each egg for 2 minutes.

4/ With a spoon or small ladle, remove the eggs from the hot water and place in cold water to stop the cooking process.

5/ Fry the cherries in a pan with a small amount of oil. Remove from heat and add the curry powder.

6/ Arrange the quails in the middle of a plate. Garnish with poached quail eggs, cherries and fennel. Season with Maldon Salt. Serve with the hot soup

Ingredients 4p

2 tbsp oil
1 carrot, coarsely chopped
1 onion, coarsely chopped
3 stalks of celery, cut into pieces
2 cups chicken stock
10 oz quail bones
(from a poultry shop)
2 quails, deboned
4 quail eggs
1 1/4 cups water
1 tbsp white vinegar
Vegetable oil
Handful cherries, pitted
5 tsp curry powder
Handful fresh wild fennel, finely chopped
Maldon Salt (flaky salt crystals)

Wine suggestion

Cuvée Rosé 2009, Pfannebecker, Rheinhessen, Germany

Davide Oldani is chef and owner of restaurant D'O in Milan. His formula caused a sensation mainly for his prices, which was very low, thanks to his choice of simple and extremely fresh ingredients in which his artisanship enhanced. D'O has one Michelin star.

Marinated Barbecued King Prawns

Neil Perry/Rockpool

Preparation

1/ Grate the lemon peel and squeeze the juice. Peel the garlic and peel and grate the ginger. Finely chop the oregano, sage and coriander. Cut the King Prawns lengthwise and open them.

2/ Crush the garlic, grated lemon, chilli flakes, ginger, oregano, sage and coriander using a mortar and pestle. Gradually add 1/2 cup of oil to form a marinade.

3/ Marinate the King Prawns for 1 hour.

4/ Heat the barbecue or grill pan.

5/ Place the open King Prawns on the barbecue or in the grill pan for 2 minutes, turning them over halfway through.

6/ Place the King Prawns on a plate, then sprinkle the grated lemon peel, oil and freshly ground pepper on top.

Ingredients 8p

1 lemon
3 cloves of garlic
small piece fresh ginger
1 tsp chilli flakes
1 tbsp finely chopped fresh oregano
1 tbsp finely chopped fresh sage
1 tbsp finely chopped fresh coriander
1/2 cup + 1 tbsp extra virgin olive oil
16 unpeeled King Prawns

Requirements

Mortar and pestle
Barbecue or grill pan

Wine suggestion

Greco di Tufo 2009,
Feudi di San Gregorio,
Kampanien, Italy

Sydney-based restaurant Rockpool, owned by Neil Perry and Trish Richards, is one of the world's leading restaurants, having received numerous awards.

Beetroot Soup with Poached Quail Eggs

Mirko Reeh/Restaurant Pearl by Mirko Reeh

Preparation

1/ Finely chop the beetroot and the onion and fry in the oil. Turn the heat up and add the condensed vegetable stock. Cook thoroughly.

2/ Purée the soup with a hand blender or blender and stir in the sour cream. Season with lemon juice, pepper, salt and ground cumin. Keep the soup warm but do not let it boil.

3/ Heat the oven to 390°F. Lay the pieces of bacon between the pieces of baking parchment or aluminium foil. Roast for 15 to 20 minutes until crispy. Drain on kitchen paper.

4/ Boil 4 1/4 cups of water. Add the vinegar and plenty of salt and reduce the heat so that the water is boiling gently. One by one, break the quail eggs open in a small ladle and slide into the boiling water. Poach for 2 minutes until done.

5/ Divide the soup among deep plates. Lay the bacon on top and then a poached quail egg. Serve immediately.

Ingredients 4p

1 lb cooked beetroot
1 onion
3 tbsp olive oil
4 1/4 cups condensed vegetable stock
1 cup sour cream
1 tsp lemon juice
1 dash of ground cumin
4 oz bacon, thinly sliced
4 quail eggs
1/4 cup white vinegar

Requirements

Hand blender or blender
Baking parchment

Wine suggestion

A dry Riesling from the Rhine region, Germany

Mirko Reeh runs 'Pearl' in Frankfurt's city centre, a gem of a place amid the blocks of banks and insurance companies. The master chef – who also runs training programmes in Frankfurt, Ibiza and Mallorca – is known for his good sense of humour, having set world records for the longest pasta and the longest Bratapfelschmandkuchen (sour cream apple cake).

Lukewarm Artichoke Salad with Herbs

Heinz Reitbauer/Steirereck Stadtpark

Preparation

1/ Mix 4 cups of water in with the lemon juice. Clean the artichokes with a serrated knife, remove the fuzz, and place the bottoms in the lemon water. Remove them from the water one by one and cut them into very thin slices. Start with the stem (8 slices for each artichoke), then drop back into the lemon water. From the remaining 'artichoke ring', cut equal-sized, small cubes and place them in the lemon water too.

2/ Cut the shallots, garlic, lemongrass and peeled ginger into thin slices. Sauté the remaining artichoke pieces in olive oil together with the shallot and the ginger. Halfway through, add garlic and lemongrass and fry until golden brown. Turn up the heat and pour in the white wine. Add the beef stock, thyme and coriander and allow to simmer for 20 minutes. Strain through a sieve and season with salt and pepper.

3/ Cook the artichoke slices in the artichoke marinade for 2 minutes and allow to soak for 30 minutes until the slices are soft. Form them into rolls and divide among 4 plates.

4/ Fry the artichoke cubes in sunflower oil until they are golden brown. At the very last minute add the 1/2 tbsp of butter. Season with salt and allow to drain on a paper towel.

5/ Reduce the artichoke marinade to 1 1/4 cups; then whisk 3 tbsp of butter through the sauce. Distribute the sauce and crunchy artichoke cubes among the artichoke rolls. Make a dressing of white wine vinegar and hazelnut oil and mix it through the herb salad. Place the salad on top of the artichoke rolls.

Ingredients 4p

12 large artichokes
2 lemons, squeezed
2 medium size shallots
2 cloves of garlic
3 tbsp olive oil
1 small piece of ginger
3 stems of lemongrass
1/2 cup white wine
1 2/3 cups beef stock
4 sprigs of thyme
1 tbsp coriander seeds, roasted
3 1/2 tbsp butter
1 tbsp sunflower oil
1 tbsp mixed herbs
1 tsp white wine vinegar
1 tbsp hazelnut oil

Wine suggestion
2007 Weissburgunder
'Tatschler' Esterhazy, Germany

Vienna's Steirereck Stadtpark is located in one of the city's most beautiful spots: in the middle of a large park, within view of the famous statue of the composer Johann Strauss. Chef Heinz Reitbauer offers the country's best contemporary fare, using ingredients from his own farm and from farmers in the surrounding area. The restaurant has two Michelin stars.

Marinated Salmon with Tamago and Spinach

Emmanuel Stroobant/Restaurant Saint Pierre

Preparation

1/ Mix the salt, sugar and green tea. Cover the bottom of a large dish with 6/16" of the salt mixture. Lay the fish in it with the skin facing down and sprinkle the rest of the mixture on top, making sure the fish is covered. Cover with cling film and let marinate in the refrigerator for 24 hours.

2/ Take the salmon out of its crust, remove the skin and cut into 1" x 1" chunks.

3/ Heat half of the oil in a saucepan. Add half of the shallots and heat for a few seconds. Sir in half of the spinach and season with salt and pepper. Put the spinach in a clean tea towel and squeeze out as much of the moisture as possible.

4/ Beat the eggs quickly with the soy sauce and the Mirin. Heat 1 tbsp of olive oil in a saucepan over a medium heat and spoon in 1/4 tbsp of the egg mixture. As soon as it's firm, roll the omelette up and leave on the side of the pan.

5/ Sprinkle the bottom of the pan with oil and pour some more of the egg mix in, taking care that it attaches to the roll that's already in the pan. Let the new layer firm up and roll it up too, so that you are building up a layered structure.

6/ Roll the omelette onto a bamboo mat, let it cool for 3-4 minutes and cut into 1" pieces.

7/ Place some spinach and a piece of salmon on each piece of omelette.

Ingredients 8p

1 whole filleted salmon with skin
2 lb salt
2 lb sugar
1/4 cup green tea
1 lb baby spinach leaves
2 medium shallots, finely chopped
2 tbsp olive oil
8 eggs
2 tbsp soy sauce
4 tbsp Mirin (Japanese sweet wine; alternatively: sweet white wine with 1 tbsp sugar)

Wine suggestion
Sauvignon Blanc – Loire Valley

At his most celebrated restaurant, Saint Pierre in Singapore, Stroobant explores a style that blends European discipline with Asian subtlety. The restaurant is the only restaurant in the city to be a member of Relais & Chateaux, and its menu continues to evolve, in line with Stroobant's style.

Tender Lobster with Melon Salad and Ham Mousse

Erik van Loo/Restaurant Parkheuvel

Preparation

1/ Make ham mousse by mixing the ham cubes and pata negra with the chicken stock and cooking until soft. Pulse in a food processor until smooth and strain the liquid. For each cup of liqiud, add 1/2 tsp of powdered gelatine and 1/4 cup of thick cream. Season with salt and pepper.

2/ Peel and seed the melon, cut into 0.2" slices and cut these into 1.6" sticks (5 per person).

3/ Make a vinaigrette by processing the melon pulp (including the seeds) in a juice extractor. Reduce the juice to a 1/2 cup and mix this with the lavender, vinegar, a few drops of honey, pepper, salt and the peanut oil.

4/ String up the lobster tail and cook in a large pot of salted water for 4 minutes, then allow to cool in ice water. Crack open the lobster and cut the tail into 4 large pieces.

Cut the claw lengthwise. Marinate the lobster with melon vinaigrette and set aside (temperature should be lukewarm).

5/ Place the slices of pata negra on cling film, squirt the ham mousse on top and form into rolls. Set aside. Once they are chilled, cut into 1.6" slices.

6/ Alternate the melon and ham rolls and arrange the lobster, sorrel and some lettuce leaves with dressing on top. Garnish with shiso cress, chervil, chives, popcorn and vinaigrette.

Note: the ingredients for the ham mousse and vinaigrette are listed in larger quantities than actually needed, since they cannot be prepared in smaller quantities.

Ingredients 4p

For the ham mousse:
5 oz cooked ham cubes
5 oz pata negra (Jamón Ibérico)
1 1/4 cups chicken stock
gelatine powder
1/4 cup thick cream
Salt and pepper

2 Canadian Lobsters (1 lb each)
2 oz ham mousse (see step 1)
1/2 lb thinly sliced pata negra
1/3 lb cooked ham
1 cantaloupe melon
2 tbsp lavender
Vinegar and honey
3/4 cup peanut oil
Lettuce leaves and sorrel leaves
Garnish: shiso cress, chervil, chives and popcorn

Requirements

Food processor, Sieve
Juice extractor

Wine suggestion

Riesling 'F' 2008, Heymann-Löwenstein, Mosel, Germany

Erik van Loo, the chef and owner of Rotterdam's two-Michelin-starred Parkheuvel, is committed to continuously perfecting his recipes.

Citrus pesto

Filippo la Mantia/Filippo la Mantia

Preparation

1/ Slice off the top and bottom of the oranges so that they can stand upright on a work surface. Cut through the peel to the flesh of the orange and, with a sharp knife, remove the pith and skin from the orange sections.

2/ Purée the orange slices in a blender or with a hand blender, along with the almonds, capers, olive oil and basil for 2 minutes until smooth.

3/ Use the citrus pesto as a sauce for pasta or as a dressing for vegetables.

Ingredients 4p

4 oranges, peeled
1 1/2 cups peeled almonds
6 tbsp salted capers
2 cups olive oil
1 bunch of basil, leaves only

Requirements

Blender or hand blender

Wine suggestion

Lacryma Christi 2009, Feudi San Gregorio, Kampanien, Italy

Filippo La Mantia's cooking style represents the unspoilt nature of his native Sicily. Currently cooking at the Hotel Majestic in Rome, he was awarded the title of 'Best Global Ambassador of Sicilian Taste' in early 2010 in the 'Best of Sicily 2010' competition.

Short Ribs Braised in Red Wine with Celery

Daniel Boulud/DANIEL

Preparation

1/ Pour the wine into a saucepan, and reduce to half its volume over a medium heat. Remove the pan from the heat.

2/ Pre-heat oven to 355°F and place a grill in the middle. Season the ribs with salt and crushed pepper. Sprinkle the ribs with flour. Place the ribs in a large casserole with hot oil and cook on both sides for 4-5 minutes until brown.

3/ Remove all but one tbsp of the fat from the pan. Sauté the vegetables and herbs over a medium heat for 5-7 minutes. Stir in the tomato purée and allow to cook for another minute. Add the reduced wine, cooked ribs and stock to the pan. Bring to a boil, cover pan, and allow to simmer in the oven for 2.5 hours.

4/ Remove cover from pan every 30 minutes and skim off the fat. Allow the ribs and stock to cool in the pan. Put the pan in the refrigerator and scrape off the fat.

5/ Heat mixture prior to use. Being careful not to let the tender meat fall apart, place meat in a pre-heated serving dish with sides and keep warm. Allow the moisture in the pan to reduce in volume to approximately 4 cups, season sauce with salt and pepper, and pour through a fine sieve.

Delicious with stewed celery and celeriac purée.

Ingredients 8p

3 bottles of dry white wine
8 beef ribs, fat removed
2 tbsp vegetable oil
1 tsp pepper corns, crushed
1 tbsp flour
10 cloves of garlic, peeled
8 large shallots, peeled and halved
2 medium-size carrots,
cut into 1" pieces
2 celery stalks, cut into 1" pieces
1 medium-size leek,
coarsely chopped
6 sprigs of parsley
2 sprigs of thyme
2 bay leafs
2 tbsp tomato purée
12 cups of unsalted or
reduced-salt beef stock,
Freshly ground white pepper

Wine suggestion

A young, strong Médoc, such as a Pauillac or Saint Julien.

Daniel Boulud is chef-owner of several award winning restaurants and the Feast and Fêtes catering company. While he hails from Lyon, France, it is in NY that he has truly mastered the dining scene and is today considered one of the most of the leading culinary authorities in America. His NY City restaurants includ Daniel, a three Michelin star Relais & Châteaux member.

24

Oven-Roasted Halibut with Rocket Purée and Parmesan Tuiles

Robert Clark/C restaurant

Preparation

1/ Preheat the oven to 350°F. Shave 8 tuiles (strips) from the wedge of cheese. Carefully lay the tuiles on a parchment-lined baking tray and bake for 3 to 4 minutes, until the cheese starts to melt. Remove tray from oven and leave the cheese on the tray to cool.

2/ To prepare the rocket purée, blanch the rocket in boiling salted water for 1 minute, then immediately refresh in ice water.

3/ Drain the leaves and pat dry with a paper towel. Purée the leaves in a blender with 1 tbsp each of stock and oil until smooth, adding a little more stock if needed for a smooth consistency. Make sure the purée does not stay in the blender too long, as the heat of the blender will give it an unpleasant colour.

4/ To prepare the halibut, preheat the oven to 400°F. Sprinkle the halibut with salt and pepper to taste. Melt the butter in the frying pan and place the fish in the pan skin-side up.

5/ Put the frying pan in the oven for 5-7 minutes and remove from oven when the fish is not quite cooked through; the heat of the frying pan will ensure the fish is perfectly done.

6/ Divide the rocket purée among four plates, place a piece of halibut on top, and garnish with the cheese tuiles. Delicious with tomatoes and olives tossed around in olive oil.

Ingredients 4p

1 large wedge of Parmesan cheese
2 cups rocket leaves
(stems removed)
1-2 tbsp vegetable stock
1 tbsp extra virgin olive oil
4 pieces of halibut 6 oz each
1 tbsp unsalted butter

The skin of the halibut should be glossy and odourless, so make sure to smell the fish before buying it.

Requirements

Baking parchment, blender, ovenproof frying pan

Wine suggestion

Chardonnay „Rossj-Bass" 2008, Angelo Gaja, Piemont, Italy

C Restaurant in Vancouver is Robert Clark's playground - it's where he uses his talent and skills to ensure that guests have a memorable dining experience. Robert's preference is for the freshest fish and seafood, which he purchases daily from outdoor markets in the Vancouver area. The restaurant has won numerous awards, both for its cuisine and for its wine menu.

25

Seared Tuna with Mango and Fennel Salad

Rose Reisman/TV Chef

Preparation

1/ Cut the mango, fennel, jicama, red and green peppers, carrot, spring onions and coriander into very small pieces and mix in a bowl.

2/ In another bowl, combine the oil with the lemon juice, rice vinegar, 1 tbsp of sesame seeds, finely chopped garlic and chilli sauce.

3/ Pour over the vegetables, mix around, and place the salad on a serving dish.

4/ Heat the grill pan. Sprinkle the tuna with salt and pepper to taste and grill the fish for 2 minutes on each side, making sure the inside is still raw. Remove from pan and cut into thin slices. Place the tuna on top of the salad.

5/ Beat the cornflour in a small saucepan together with the soy sauce and the maple syrup until it has dissolved completely. Bring to a boil while stirring, until the cornflour has thickened the mixture.

Pour the sauce over the fish and sprinkle with the remaining sesame seeds.

Ingredients 4p

1 mango
1 bulb of fennel
1 cup jicama
1 red pepper
1 small green pepper
1 small carrot
2 spring onions
1/2 bunch of fresh coriander leaves
1 tbsp olive oil
2 tbsp lemon juice
1 tbsp rice vinegar
2 tbsp roasted sesame seeds
1 clove of garlic
1/2 tbsp hot chilli sauce
1 lb 2 oz raw tuna steaks
2 tbsp soy sauce
2 tbsp maple syrup
1 tbsp cornflour

Requirements

Grill pan

Wine suggestion

Costières de Nîmes „Terre d'Argence" Blanc 2008, Château Mourgues du Grès, Languedoc, France

Since publishing her breakthrough cookbook Rose Reisman Brings Home Light Cooking in 1993, Reisman has enjoyed success as a food writer, caterer, TV presenter and in many other areas. She taught cooking to packed audiences for many years and has published 16 books.

26

Spring Dish with Cabbage and Bacon

Magnus Ek/Oaxen Skärgårdskrog

Preparation

1/ Cut the bacon into pieces of approximately 1" x 2" in. Cut the spring cabbage into pieces, slice the potatoes and chop the garlic and parsley finely. Chop the shallots.

2/ Put the bacon, spring cabbage, potatoes, garlic and stock in a pan, bring to a boil and cook until the potatoes start to crumble.

3/ Add the butter, shallot and parsley, heat up again and season with salt and a drop of vinegar. Serve with mustard.

Ingredients 4p

7 oz smoked bacon
1 spring cabbage
1 lb 9 oz potatoes
1 clove of garlic
8 1/2 cups chicken stock
(preferably made with pig's ear mushrooms added)
5 tbsp butter
4 shallots
1/2 bunch parsley
Vinegar
Whole-grain mustard

Wine suggestion

Spätburgunder 2008,
Theo Minges, Pfalz, Germany

One of Sweden's most influential chefs, Magnus Ek gained fame through his optimisation process, which he introduced a decade ago. In his restaurant Oaxen Skärgårdskrog he uses ingredients from local organic farms and applies traditional techniques to preserve them. During the winter months, he closes his restaurant and completely updates the menu.

27

Corn-Fed Chicken Stuffed with Tarragon and Ricotta

Tim Mälzer/Bullerei

Preparation

1/ With a sharp knife, carefully cut the corn-fed chicken fillets deeply on one side.

2/ In a bowl, season the ricotta with tarragon, nutmeg, salt and pepper to taste, and mix into a smooth paste together with the breadcrumbs. Preheat oven to 392°F.

3/ Stuff the fillets with the ricotta mixture and season with salt and pepper.

4/ Fry the fillets in the oil, skin-side down, until golden brown (4-5 minutes). Tip: if the stuffing leaks out, continue frying the chicken fillets in the pan on top of the stuffing. Pour off the frying fat and allow fillets to roast in the oven on the other side for another 10 minutes.

5/ Heat the remaining oil in a frying pan and fry the asparagus slices at a high heat together with the dried tomatoes for 3-4 minutes. Season with salt, pepper and sugar and serve together with the chicken fillets.

Ingredients 4p

4 corn-fed chicken fillets (6 oz each)
1 cup ricotta
2 tbsp breadcrumbs
3 tbsp fresh tarragon, finely chopped
Dash of nutmeg
2 tbsp olive oil
1 lb 10 oz white or green asparagus, peeled and sliced diagonally
1/2 cup dried tomatoes, roughly chopped
Sugar

Wine suggestion

Sauvignon Blanc 'Steirische Klassik' 2008, Sattlerhof, Südsteiermark, Austria

The renowned German chef, TV celebrity and cookbook author Tim Mälzer opened his restaurant, Bullerei, in Hamburg in July 2009.

28

Seven-Hour Lamb

Tom Aikens/Tom's Kitchen

Preparation

1/ Heat the oven to 210°F and heat the two types of stock.

2/ Heat 6 tbsp of oil in a large, thick-bottomed pan. Sprinkle the lamb with salt and pepper. Put the meat in the pan once the oil is very hot and cook in 2-3 minutes until brown all over. Remove the meat from the pan and pour away most of the fat.

3/ Peel and crush 3 cloves of garlic and put the meat back into the pan. Add the thyme (setting some aside) and crushed garlic and cook for another 1-2 minutes.

4/ Add 5 tbsps of sugar and 1 1/4 cups of balsamic vinegar, then reduce the mixture to half its volume. Add the two types of hot stock (setting 1/3 cup of each type aside) and place the covered pan in the oven. Cook for 7 hours until the meat is done.

5/ Trim away the outer layer of the shallots without removing the root end. Slice the shallots as far as the root, ensuring it remains intact while cooking. Sprinkle with salt and pepper to taste. Heat the remaining oil in a saucepan and fry the shallots until golden brown.

6/ Mix the butter and bay leaves with the remaining crushed garlic, thyme and sugar, and cook the shallots for another 5 minutes while stirring.

7/ Pour in the remaining balsamic vinegar and the rest of the two types of stock. Reduce mixture to 2/3 of its volume in 20-30 minutes. Season with salt and pepper. Serve the shallots with the shoulder of lamb.

Ingredients 4p

1 shoulder of lamb
1/2 bunch of thyme
6 tbsp oil
6 cloves of garlic
2 cups good-quality balsamic vinegar
6 tbsp brown caster sugar
4 1/4 cups chicken stock
4 1/4 cups veal stock
5 shallots
1 tbsp butter
3 bay leafs

Wine suggestion

Viñas de Gain Tinto 2006,
Artadi, Rioja, Spain

Undeniably one of Britain's most exciting chefs, Tom Aikens established his culinary reputation after opening his own restaurant in Chelsea, London in April 2003. The low-key restaurant, which seats just 60 people, has received numerous awards, including a Michelin star.

29

Rice with Pork

Rudi and Karl Obauer/Obauer

Preparation

1/ Dice the onions and cut the meat into thin slices. Heat the lard in a thick-bottomed pan and sauté the onions and meat in the pan. Add the stock. Crush the garlic and add it, along with the bay leaf, paprika powder, caraway and rice. Cook the mix on a low heat for 30 minutes. Add one piece of pork rind and cheese rind for flavour (optional).

2/ Cut the peppers into cubes and finely slice the pickles and chilli peppers. When the rice is almost done, add the peppers, pickles and chilli peppers and stir.

3/ Remove the pork rind and the cheese rind. Season the rice dish with salt and sprinkle Parmesan and fresh herbs over it. Add chopped capers and some olive oil if you wish (optional). Serve with salad.

Ingredients 6p

3 tbsp (pork) lard
2 onions
1 lb 9 oz organic pork fillet
3 cups beef stock
1 bay leaf
3 tbsp mild paprika powder
3 cloves of garlic, crushed
1 dash of cayenne pepper
1 dash of ground caraway seeds
2 cups long-grain rice
2 red peppers
2 dill pickles
2 chilli peppers (optional)
1/2 cup grated Parmesan cheese
1 tbsp fresh herbs, chopped
(e.g. chervil, wild garlic, chives, marjoram, one leaf of sage)
Optional: pork rind
Rind of Parmesan cheese
2 tbsp capers and olive oil

Wine suggestion

A Sauvignon Blanc, or a glass of good-quality beer.

Brothers Rudi and Karl Obauer have been working together since 1979. That year, Karl took over the family business, while Rudolf gained international experience by training with several leading European chefs. The siblings have continuously improved the restaurant over the years and restored the historic building, which has brought them countless awards and prizes, as well as two Michelin stars.

30

Jason's Burgers

Jason Atherton/TV Chef

Preparation

1/ Preheat oven to 180°F.

2/ Cut the ciabatta lengthwise. Crush 4 cloves of garlic and finely chop the other one. Soak the dried chilli peppers and chop them finely.

3/ Sprinkle the open ciabatta with oil; rub the inside with paprika powder and crushed garlic. Bake the bread on an oven rack for 5 minutes until golden brown. In a bowl, mix the gound beef, the finely chopped garlic, chilli, spring onion, egg and breadcrumbs and season with salt and pepper. Form into four flat balls.

3/ Heat a grill pan over medium heat and grill the burgers for 5 minutes on each side (or longer if preferred). Cut the ciabatta into four pieces and divide the burgers among them.

4/ Garnish with lettuce, tomatoes, red onion and ketchup.

Ingredients 4p

1-2 tbsp olive oil
1 ciabatta
Dash of paprika powder
(smoked if preferred)
5 cloves of garlic
1 lb 2 oz ground beef
2 dried chilli peppers
(preferably chipotles)
4-5 spring onions, cut into rings
1 egg, lightly beaten
3 tbsp breadcrumbs
4 leaves of lettuce
2 tomatoes, sliced
1/2 red onion, cut into half-rings
4 tbsp ketchup

Requirements

Grill pan

Wine suggestion

Zinfandel 2007, Seghesio Family Vineyards, California, USA

British chef Jason Atherton has had a long and varied career. While backpacking in Spain in 1998, he took an unpaid job at the celebrated three-Michelin-starred restaurant El Bulli, run by chef Ferran Adrià. After a spell at Gordon Ramsay's Maze upon his return to London in 2005, he opened his own restaurant this year.

31

Scallops, Chanterelles and Chicory with Mushroom Risotto

Jean Michel Lorain/La Cote Saint Jacques

Preparation

1/ In a small pan, heat 2 tbsp of butter and use this to fry the chanterelle heads. Add salt and pepper to taste.

2/ Remove the heads and drop the stems into the pan. Add the stock and reduce at a low heat.

3/ Sieve the liquid through a Chinois (cone-shaped sieve) and whisk in 2 tbsp of cold butter cubes in order to allow the sauce to thicken. Add salt and pepper to taste.

4/ Cut the chicory into very thin strips, cover pot, and cook on a very low flame in some butter, a tbsp of lemon juice, and salt, pepper and sugar to taste.

5/ Heat the remaining butter and clarify it by removing the egg protein that forms on top. Cut star shapes from the filo dough and bake them in a frying pan with clarified butter until golden brown.

6/ Chop a few celery leaves into small pieces. Season the scallops with salt and pepper and cook them at a high heat in the clarified butter.

7/ Heat the milk and whisk until frothy.

8/ Then place a small mound of mushrooms in the middle of a deep plate.

9/ Arrange the scallops around the mushrooms. Garnish each scallop with a few chicory strips and a filo pastry star. Pour the warm mushroom sauce into the plate. Top with a few dots of milk foam, a dash of cocoa powder and some finely chopped celery.

Ingredients 4p

10 tbsp butter
6 cups (14 oz) chanterelles, cleaned; separate the stems and heads
1 chicory
1 strip of filo pastry dough, defrosted
1 stalk of celery
3/4 cup chicken stock
Juice of half a lemon
1/2 tsp sugar
20 scallops, cleaned
1/2 cup milk
1 tsp Cocoa powder

Requirements

Chinois (cone-shaped sieve)

Wine suggestion

Benefizium Porer Pinot Grigio, 2008, Alois Lageder, Alto Adige, Italy

Free spirit Jean-Michel Lorain has used his creative powers to reach the highest culinary standards, always respecting the flavour of each ingredient. All the leading restaurant guides have hailed Lorain as one of the best chefs of his generation; he is the recipient of 19 Gault Millau points and three Michelin stars.

32

Oven-Roasted Garlic Chicken

Anthony Sedlak/TV Chef

Preparation

1/ In a large pan, mix 3 cups of water, the wine, celery, half an onion, 10 cloves of crushed garlic, sugar, salt the white peppercorns, bay leafs, the sprigs of parsley and one sprig of thyme. Bring to a boil then allow to cool.

2/ Place the chicken in the liquid, making sure it is completely covered, and place in the refrigerator overnight.

3/ Preheat oven to 400°F. Remove the chicken from the liquid and pat it dry. Sieve the vegetables and herbs from the liquid (you will no longer need the liquid).

4/ Loosen the chicken skin and spread half of the butter across the chicken under the skin, then distribute 2 finely chopped cloves of garlic beneath the skin. Mix the fresh herbs with the boiled vegetables and herbs and use this to stuff the chicken. Use the remaining butter to spread on the outside of the chicken and season with salt and pepper to taste.

5/ Spread the onion across an oiled oven dish and place the chicken on top. Cut off the tops of the garlic bulbs, place them next to the chicken and sprinkle the remaining oil on top. Roast the chicken for approximately 1 hour, until the juices run clear. Cover the chicken with tinfoil and allow it to sit for 15 minutes before carving.

Ingredients 4p

3 cups white wine
1 celery stalk, chopped
1 1/2 onion, chopped
12 cloves of garlic, peeled and crushed
2 bulbs of garlic
2 tbsp white peppercorns
6 bay leafs
9 sprigs of parsley
3 sprigs of thyme
1/4 cup sugar
1/4 cup salt
1 chicken (3 - 3 1/2 lb)
4 tbsp soft butter
1/4 cup olive oil

Wine suggestion

Chardonnay "234" 2009, Enate, Somontano, Spain

Canadian-born chef Anthony L. Sedlak first gained national fame as a TV presenter. Ever since winning a silver medal at the Hans Bueschken World Junior Chef Challenge in Auckland at the age of 22, Anthony's career has been on a roll. After being involved in the launch of the Vancouver-based Corner Suite Bistro De Luxe, he has been focusing on other new, challenging projects.

33

Fricassee of Wels Catfish with Horseradish and Julienne Vegetables

Heinz Winkler/Residenz Heinz Winkler

Preparation

1/ Let the catfish sit in ice water for one day to allow it to relax and ensure it has a juicier taste. Fillet the fish, remove its skin, and cut the fish into pieces of 1.5" x 1.5".

2/ Cut the carrot, celery and leeks into strips and cook each of these vegetables separately in salted water for 2-3 minutes. Drain the vegetables.

3/ Bring the white wine and Noilly Prat to a boil and add the condensed fish stock. Reduce by one-third and melt the butter into the mixture. Season the sauce with salt, pepper and white wine (optional). Add the vegetable strips to the water very briefly at the last minute.

4/ Poach the fish by bringing the stock to a near boil and placing the fish in it for 3-5 minutes. Remove the fish pieces and pat dry.

5/ Divide the sauce among the preheated plates and place the pieces of fish on top. For each portion, slice 5 thin strips off the peeled horseradish (using a vegetable peeler if possible) and arrange them between the pieces of fish. Garnish with watercress.

Ingredients 4p

One 4 lb 7 oz wels catfish that you clean yourself, or a firm white fish such as cod cleaned by the fishmonger; approx. 1/3 lb per person
6 medium carrots
5 strips celery
2 leeks
1/2 cup dry white wine
1/4 cup Noilly Prat (vermouth)
1 shallot, shredded
2 cups condensed fish stock
12 tbsp of butter
4 cups fish stock
1 chunk of fresh horseradish (or cucumber)
A few watercress leaves

Wine suggestion
A Sancerre or Sauvignon

The three-Michelin-starred chef Heinz Winkler, who is also the author of several cookbooks, selected this dish because it is both delicious and very easy to prepare.

34

Roasted Pork Ribs with Summer Vegetable Vinaigrette and Herb Salad

Ronald Kunis/Restaurant De Kas

Preparation

1/ Stick the sprigs of rosemary between the meat strings.

2/ Crush the garlic and mix with 5 tbsp of oil. Season with salt and pepper and brush it over the meat. Allow flavours to blend for four hours, then roast the meat over a charcoal fire until done.

3/ Shred the shallots. Grate and squeeze the lemon.

4/ Cook the legumes separately for 2-4 minutes until tender, mix with the oil, shallots, lemon peel and lemon juice, and season with salt and pepper.

5/ Sprinkle each plate with fresh herbs to taste, then add slices of roast pork rib with some legume salad on top.

Ingredients 6p

Sprigs of fresh rosemary
2 lb 3 oz pork rib, tied up by butcher
5 tbsp olive oil
2 cloves of garlic
2 cups Fava beans, pods removed
4 cups of shelled peas
2/3 cup olive oil
2 medium shallots
1 lemon
Seasoning to taste (for example, tips of basil, chervil, tarragon, chives or violet leaves)

Requirements

Charcoal Fire

Wine suggestion

Cuvée Lairis 2007, Jean-Luc Matha, Marcillac, France

The 50,000 guests this restaurant attracts annually love it for its relaxed setting in the middle of Amsterdam's Frankendaelpark, the 19th-century architecture of the surrounding Watergraafsmeer district and the fresh herbs and vegetables grown in the restaurant's own nursery.

35

Papillote of Fish with Mini-Leeks, Juniper Berry Butter and Grated Lemon Peel

Anne-Sophie Pic/Maison Pic

Preparation

1/ Preheat oven to 355°F.

2/ Work the butter into a cream and add the finely chopped juniper berries. Divide the mixture between two sheets of greaseproof paper. Place mixture in refrigerator.

3/ Wash the baby leeks. Cook them for 3 minutes, then immediately immerse them in cold water. Drain well and place them on a large sheet of greaseproof paper.

4/ Sprinkle the pieces of fish with salt to taste, place them on top of the mini leeks, and spread the juniper berry butter on top. Fold the paper into a papillote and bake in the oven for 5-7 minutes, depending on the thickness of the fish.

5/ Open the package, then garnish the fish with thin strips of grated lemon peel. Sprinkle with sea salt to taste.

Ingredients 4p

3 1/2 tbsp soft butter
6 juniper berries, finely chopped
12 thin baby leeks
1 tbsp organic grated lemon peel
4 pieces of red mullet, gurnard, sea perch or Atlantic croaker (4 oz each)
Sea salt to taste

Requirements

Greaseproof paper

Wine suggestion

Saint Péray Pic Chapoutier 2008

This quick, easy recipe first appeared in a book by this French-born chef. As the first woman to be awarded the title of 'Chef of the Year' by the Michelin Guide, Anne-Sophie Pic beat eight thousand other master chefs. Pic is the chef at La Maison Pic in Valence, which her family has owned since 1934. Grandfather André, father Jacques and daughter Anne-Sophie have three Michelin stars between them.

36

Potato Gnocchi with Porcini Mushrooms, Oven-Roasted Tomatoes and Curly Leaf Parsley

Harald Wohlfahrt/Schwarzwaldstube in Hotel Traube Tonbach

Preparation

1/ Wash the potatoes and boil them (unpeeled) in salted water until tender. Peel the potatoes while they are still hot.

2/ Rub the potatoes through a sieve then carefully mix in the egg, flour, salt, ground pepper and nutmeg. The mixture should remain light and airy.

3/ Form the still-warm dough into rolls with a thickness of 0.6". Carefully slice the rolls into 0.8" long pieces; use these to make 48 gnocchi and press them lightly with a fork.

4/ Clean the mushrooms, brush them under running water, and pat them dry with a paper towel. Cut the mushrooms lengthwise.

5/ Melt the butter in a pan, then add the thyme and the crushed garlic cloves. Add the mushrooms and sauté them until golden brown. Then add the vegetable stock and bring to a boil. Just before serving, add the diced tomatoes and finely chopped parsley.

5/ Bring a pan of salted water to a boil and add the gnocchi. Carefully remove the gnocchi as soon as they float to the top, and add them to the pan with the mushrooms. Heat mixture while stirring and season to taste. Divide the pan's contents among several deep plates and serve immediately.

Ingredients 4p

1 lb 3 oz mealy potatoes

1 1/4 cups of flour

1 egg

Dash of nutmeg

1 lb porcini mushrooms

7 tbsp clarified butter

1 shallot, finely chopped

2 cloves of garlic

1 bunch of curly leaf parsley, finely chopped

1 sprig of thyme

1 cup condensed vegetable stock

1 1/2 cups of canned diced tomatoes

Wine suggestion

DWeissburgunder + Chardonnay from the Johner Estate in Bischoffingen, or another Pinot Blanc.

One of the most celebrated chefs in Europe, Harald Wohlfahrt is the recipient of three Michelin stars and 19 Gault Millau points.

37

Ginger and Orange Beef

Michael Smith/Ocean Entertainment

Preparation

1/ Cut the stewing steak into pieces, shred the onions and slice the ginger into thin pieces.

2/ Heat the oil in a frying pan on a medium flame. Sprinkle the meat with salt and pepper to taste and cook until brown all over. Remove the meat from the pan.

3/ Sauté the onions and ginger until brown, adding water if necessary. Pour in the stock and the orange juice.

4/ Add the meat, marmalade, soy sauce and 5-spice powder. Bring to a boil and reduce the heat to the lowest setting. Cover and allow to simmer for at for at least one hour. Add salt and pepper to taste.

5/ Divide the spinach and bean sprouts among four bowls. Stir the spring onions and half of the coriander through the casserole; then divide the meat among the bowls. Garnish with the remaining cilantro.

Ingredients 4p

2 tbsp oil
1 lb of stewing steak
2 onions
small piece of unpeeld ginger
1 can beef stock (1 1/4 cups)
1 cup orange juice
1 cup orange marmalade
1 tbsp soy sauce
1 tbsp 5-spice powder
1 bag fresh baby
spinach leaves (10 oz)
A handful of bean sprouts
1 bunch of green onions, chopped
A handful of cilantro leaves

Wine suggestion
Sankt Laurant 2008, Weingut
Schumacher, Pfalz, Germany

A winner of the James Beard Award for Cooking Show Excellence, Canada's leading chef Michael Smith presents the popular TV shows Chef at Home, Chef at Large and The Inn Chef on Food Network Canada, which are broadcast in 26 countries. He has contributed this delicious dish to the book.

38

Marinated Black Pollack with Mango-Papaya Chutney

Stefan Stiller/Stiller's restaurant

Preparation

1/ Mix all the ingredients for the marinade together and add the fish filet. Marinate the fish for at least 1 hour but no longer than 5 hours.

2/ Mix the ingredients for the chutney together and season with salt and pepper. The chutney can be spicy, but not too hot. Remove the fish from the marinade.

3/ Preheat the oven to 320°F. Heat the oil in a non-stick frying pan and quickly fry the fish until brown on both sides, taking care not to burn the soy sauce. Cook the fish in the oven for 8-10 minutes until done. Serve with the chutney.

Ingredients 4p

For the marinade:

3.53 oz ginger, finely chopped

6 cloves of garlic, finely chopped

1/2 cup dark soy sauce

1/2 cup sesame oil

1 hot chilli

A handful of coriander chopped

1 tbsp black sesame seeds

1 lb 5 oz Black Pollack (also known as Coalfish or Saithe)

For the chutney:

1 1/2 cups mango, finely chopped

1 1/2 cups papaya, finely chopped

1 shallot, finely chopped

1 red chilli pepper, finely chopped

1/4 cup fresh orange juice

1 tbsp fresh lime juice

2 tbsp olive oil

Wine suggestion

Montlouis "Les Choisilles" 2007,
Domaine Francois Chidaine,
Loire, France

Stefan Stiller learned his trade at Michelin-starred restaurants such as Goldener Pflug in Cologne and first became head chef at the Deidesheimer Hof. The world has been at his feet ever since. He opened his own restaurant The Grand Cru and has been working in Shanghai since 2005, where he and his wife, Yoshi, established Club Shanghai and the Mimosa Supper Club, both a tremendous success.

39

Jerusalem Artichoke Risotto with Poached Lobster and Sage Butter

David Laris/Laris

Preparation

1/ Bring a large pot of water to a boil and season liberally with salt. Lay the lobsters on a cutting board, insert the point of a sharp kitchen knife between the eyes and plunge the knife in deeply. Remove the lobster's claws and tail with your hands or with a knife. Cook the claws for 3 1/2 minutes, the tail for 5 minutes and the lobster itself for 5-7 minutes. Allow to cool in a pan of ice cold water, then remove the meat from the shell.

2/ Mix 12 oz of soft butter with the sage, season with salt, wrap in cling film and allow to firm.

3/ Heat 3 1/2 tbsp of butter in a pan on a low flame and stir in the Jerusalem artichoke. Cook for 8-10 minutes, then purée with a fork and season.

4/ In a thick-bottomed pan, sauté the onion in 3 1/2 tbsp of butter until translucent. Add the rice and stir until each grain is covered with a coating of butter. Turn up the heat, add the wine and continue to stir until all the liquid is absorbed. Add a cup of chicken stock, continue to stir, and add the next cup only when the last has been completely absorbed by the rice. After 10 minutes, stir in the puréed Jerusalem artichoke and continue to add the stock until the rice is creamy and cooked al dente.

5/ Turn the heat down low, stir in the Parmesan, 2 tbsp of butter and Mascarpone, and season with salt and parsley. Meanwhile, heat the lobster in the remaining butter.

6/ Serve the risotto with the lobster, sage butter, rocket and lemon.

Ingredients 6-8p

3 lobsters, 3 lbs each
1 lb 2 oz butter
2 tbsp finely chopped sage
5 cups Jerusalem artichoke, peeled and cubed
1 onion, finely chopped
2 1/2 cups Arborio rice
3/4 cup dry white wine
8 1/2 cups of chicken stock
1/2 cup Parmesan cheese, grated
2 tbsp Mascarpone cheese
1 tbsp finely chopped parsley
Rocket for garnish
1 lemon, cut into wedges

Wine suggestion

Gavi di Gavi "Monterotondo" 2007, Villa Sparina, Piemont, Italy

One of the best-known and most prolific restaurateurs in Shanghai, David Laris is the man behind The Fat Olive, Martini Bar, Slice, the Barbie Cafe, The Opposite House in Beijing and Laris, his restaurant in Three on the Bund.

40

Fusilli with White Grouper and Sweet-and-Sour Lime Sauce

Gennaro Esposito/Torre del Saracino

Preparation

1/ Cut through the lime peel to the flesh. Then, with a sharp knife, cut the pulp out of the section skins.

2/ Heat 1 tbsp of oil and sauté 1 finely chopped clove of garlic. Add the lime pieces and bring to a boil. Season with candied lime peel, salt and pepper.

3/ Heat the remaining oil and sauté the rest of the garlic in it. Add thyme, parsley and stock and reduce on a low flame; season with salt and pepper.

4/ Cook the fusilli al dente in a large pot of boiling salted water. Stir in the pasta with the grouper sauce, add the sliced grouper fillet, and mix the ingredients together over a high heat.

5/ Garnish with drops of lime sauce. Decorate the dish with finely sliced pieces of candied tomato.

Ingredients 4p

1 lime
1/2 cup extra virgin olive oil
(preferably DOP Penisola Sorrentina)
2 cloves of garlic
1/2 cup of candied lime peel (you can grate the peel yourself and candy it in a small amount of sugar syrup)
2 cups fusilli pasta
1 sprig of thyme
1 tbsp finely diced flat-leaf parsley
1 cup grouper stock or regular fish stock
7.05 oz grouper or sea bass filet
2 tbsp candied tomatoes or semi-dried tomatoes

Wine suggestion
Fiano di Avellino

In 1992, Gennaro Esposito opened his restaurant 'La Torre del Saracino', which offers guests a stunning view over the Bay of Naples. In addition to receiving its first Michelin star in 2001 and a second one in 2008, it has won a broad range of other awards. Esposito uses only high-quality local ingredients, including fruit from his own garden.

Oven-Roasted Chicken with Olives and Capers

Tetsuya Wakuda/Tetsuya's restaurant

Preparation

1/ Preheat oven to 390°F.

2/ Place the chicken halves in the oven dish skin-side up; season with salt and pepper. Pour in the wine until it comes up to the middle of the chicken.

3/ Add the capers, olives, garlic and oregano, sprinkle the oil on top and roast the chicken in approximately 45 minutes.

4/ Serve the chicken with some of the cooking juices and sprinkle with parsley.

Ingredients 4p

4 half chickens

1 cup dry white wine

2 tbsp salted capers, rinsed

20 black olives

4 cloves of garlic, finely chopped

1/2 tbsp oregano, chopped

1/2 cup olive oil

1 tbsp fresh parsley, finely chopped

Requirements

Large oven dish

Wine suggestion

Tyrrell's Hunter Semillion 2002 or a Curly Flat Pinot Noir, Macedon Ranges, VIC Australia

In his Sydney-based restaurant, Tetsuya combines the Japanese philosophy of natural, seasonal flavours with classic French techniques and the freshest possible ingredients. This places him among a select group of top chefs who have inspired many of their peers across the world.

Puff Pastry with Fresh Fruit, Vanilla Mousse and Chocolate Sauce

Yo Saumande/Auberge Michel

Preparation

1/ Preheat oven to 355°F and bake the puff pastry for 12-15 minutes until golden brown. Allow to cool.

2/ Meanwhile, bring the milk and a cut-open vanilla bean to the boil. Mix the eggs with half of the sugar, then stir in the flour. Add the mixture to the boiling milk and allow to cook for 2 minutes longer. Let the mixture cool.

3/ Allow the butter to soften and beat 7 tbsp through the milk mixture.

4/ Boil the other half of the sugar with 1/4 cup of water for 1 minute and allow to cool.

5/ Place a large bowl in a pan of boiling water (au bain marie). Put in 3 tbsp of butter, the cream, the chocolate chopped into small pieces and the sugar water, and let it melt completely.

6/ Cut the half pineapple and the strawberries into pieces.

7/ Place a piece of puff pastry on a plate, spoon some vanilla mousse and fresh fruit on top, and cover with another piece of puff pastry. Serve with the chocolate sauce.

This dessert also combines well with all kinds of seasonal fruit. The cream can be prepared the day before if you wish.

Ingredients 5p

1 cup milk
3 tbsp flour
1/2 cup sugar
2 eggs
1 vanilla bean
10 tbsp soft butter
9 oz puff pastry, in 10 squares
1/2 cup cream
3/4 cup grated dark chocolate
1/2 pineapple
2 cups Muscat grapes
2 cups strawberries

Wine suggestion

Nitida Weisser Riesling Noble late harvest

Johannesburg's Auberge Michel, which was an immediate hit when it first opened its doors in April 2004, is highly acclaimed in South Africa for its superior French cuisine and impeccable service.

44

Yogurt Mousse with Almond Biscuits and Raspberries

Andreas Caminada/Schloss Schauenstein

Preparation

1/ Preheat oven to 355°F.

2/ Beat the egg white in a clean bowl together with 1/2 cup of sugar until stiff peaks form.

3/ Blend the ground almonds and the remaining, followed by the melted butter. Spoon the mix into a biscuit mould* on a silicone baking mat and bake for 10 minutes. With a knife, carefully separate the biscuits from the mould.

4/ Mix together the crème fraîche, yogurt and icing sugar. Heat the gelatine in a small amount of the yogurt mixture until dissolved and blend it with the rest of the mixture. Season with lemon and lime juice and stir well. Blend the whipped cream together with the mixture and spoon into a baking dish. Let it cool for 2 hours in the refrigerator.

5/ Marinate the raspberries in the icing sugar, raspberry liqueur and a small amount of raspberry purée.

6/ Cut the chilled yogurt mousse into nice-sized portions and divide among the plates. Place raspberries on top. Sprinkle the almond cookies with icing sugar and put them on the mousse as decoration. Would go well with a berry sorbet.

* You can easily make a biscuit mould from thin cardboard. Cut out the desired shapes, soak in olive oil and rinse with water.

Ingredients 4p

1/2 cup fresh egg white
1 1/4 cups sugar
1 1/2 cups ground almonds
1 1/2 tbsp melted butter
1/2 cup yogurt
1/2 cup crème fraîche
1/2 cup icing sugar, sifted
1 1/2 tsp of gelatine powder
The juice of 1 lemon
The juice of 1 lime
1 1/2 cups whipped cream
Raspberries to taste
Raspberry liqueur

Requirements

Silicone baking mat or baking parchment

Wine suggestion

Brachetto Teodora 2008, Tenuta il Falchetto, Piemont, Italy

Schloss Schauenstein had been a well-kept secret among foodies, but that all changed when the Swiss restaurant's chef, Andreas Caminada, was named Discovery of the Year 2005 by Gault-Millau. It's no wonder, as the former castle in the Domleschg Valley looks like something straight out of a James Bond film. Caminada's cooking, too, is nothing short of spectacular, as should be evident from his restaurant's 19 Gault Millau points and two Michelin stars.

45

Stewed Pears with Acacia Honey and Cardamom, filled with Chantilly Cream

Luca Montersino/Golosi di Salute

Preparation

1/ Heat the honey, sugar, cinnamon, vanilla and cardamom together with 5 cups of water. Allow to boil for 5 minutes.

2/ Peel the pears, without removing the stems. Add the peeled pears and allow to simmer, pot covered, for 25 minutes. Allow the pears to cool, then cut them in half and remove the pulp. Cut the pulp into small cubes and add them to the cooking juices. Reduce the mixture by half.

3/ Place the pears in a bowl and fill them with the pear cubes, biscuit pieces and Chantilly cream.

4/ Place in freezer. Bring the cream to a boil, melt the chocolate into it and use this mixture to cover the pears.

5/ Serve the pears together with the reduced liquid. You can garnish the plate with the spices used, if you wish.

Ingredients 4p

1 3/4 cups honey
3 cups refined granulated sugar
4 large pears
1 cinnamon stick
1 vanilla stick
2 cardamom pods
2 1/2 cups unwhipped cream
8 biscuits, crumbed
5 bars dark chocolate (2.5 oz each), broken into pieces
2 cups whipped cream

Wine suggestion

Suprême de Thou 2004,
Henri Lapouble-Laplace,
Jurançon, France

One of Italy's most acclaimed pastry chefs, Luca Montersino is the former director of Venice's l'Etoile restaurant. He is renowned as a great connoisseur of Italian cuisine.

46

Caramelised Apple Tarte Tatin with Vanilla Ice Cream

Gordon Ramsay/Restaurant Gordon Ramsay

Preparation

1/ Peel the apples, remove the cores and cut each apple into 4 pieces. Place them on a baking tray covered with a paper towel. Leave to dry for 2 to 3 hours, uncovered, or chill overnight. It is fine if the apples turn brown, as they will be covered with a layer of caramel later.

2/ Roll the dough onto a work surface sprinkled with flour until you have a thin slab; then, using a plate, cut a 2" circle. Place the circle of dough onto a baking tray and chill.

3/ Preheat oven to 320°F. Spread the butter across the bottom of the pan and sprinkle with sugar. Neatly arrange the apple slices along the edge of the pan, placing one slice in the middle. Place in the oven until the butter and the sugar are melted and a light caramel has formed.

4/ Shake the pan occasionally to ensure the apples turn brown all over and are well covered with the caramel. Allow to cool a little.

5/ Heat oven to 390°F. Cover the apples in the pan with the puff pastry and bake the tarte tatin for another 15-20 minutes until the dough is golden brown and crispy. Allow to cool.

6/ Liberally sprinkle the remaining vanilla beans with icing sugar and shake off the excess sugar. Slide the tarte tatin onto a deep plate. Place the sugar-sprinkled vanilla beans on top and serve with scoops of vanilla ice cream.

Ingredients 2-4p

2-4 servings vanilla ice cream
3 large, crunchy apples
(Pink Lady or similar)
2 vanilla beans, cut open
1 cup refined sugar
9 oz puff pastry (frozen), defrosted
3 1/2 tbsp cold, unsalted butter, thinly sliced
Icing sugar to sprinkle on top

Requirements

Shallow ovenproof pan
(with a diameter of 8")

Wine suggestion

Riesling Auslese 2008, Pfannebecker, Rheinhessen, Germany

The world-renowned chef Gordon Ramsay has been awarded numerous Michelin stars, as well as gaining fame through his TV shows Kitchen Nightmares and Hell's Kitchen.

47

Chocolate Fudge Cake

Michael Caines/Gidleigh Park

Preparation

1/ Preheat the oven to 320°F. Melt the chocolate in a bowl suspended above a pot of boiling water, making sure the bottom of the bowl does not touch the water.

2/ In a food processor, mix one cup of butter with 2 1/2 cups of caster sugar until white and creamy. While the food processor is running, add the egg yolks one by one, followed by the ground almonds. Transfer the mixture to a bowl and stir in the chocolate, followed by the breadcrumbs and flour.

3/ In a separate bowl, beat the egg whites with a pinch of salt until they form stiff peaks. Carefully fold the eggs through the chocolate mixture and transfer this to the spring form. Bake for 1 hour until done.

4/ Put the cocoa powder and icing sugar into a mixing bowl. Heat 1/2 cup of butter with 1 cup of caster sugar and 6 tbsp of water until completely dissolved. Stir this through the dry mixture in the bowl and blend until the mixture is thick and somewhat liquid. Add the vanilla bean scrapings, then pour the mixture over the cooled-down chocolate cake. Make sure the entire top is covered, then leave to cool.

Ingredients 12p

8 oz dark chocolate
1 1/2 cups unsalted butter
3 1/2 cups caster sugar
6 eggs, whites and yolks separated
1 1/4 cups ground almonds
1 1/2 cups white breadcrumbs
1/4 cup flour
Scrapings of 2 vanilla beans
3 tsp or 1 envelope (3oz) cocoa powder
2 cups icing sugar

Requirements

Food processor
Spring form (with a diameter of 10"), greased and lined with baking parchment

Wine suggestion

Pedro Ximenez Gran Réserva 1982, Bodegas Toro Albalá, Cordoba, Spain

Gidleigh Park in Dartmoor, Devon has been the proud owner of two Michelin stars for a decade now.
The restaurant, headed by chef Michael Caines, is renowned for its innovative European cuisine.

48

Strawberry meringue tarts

Anna Olson/TV Chef

Preparation

1/ Mix the flour with 1 1/2 tbsp of sugar and a pinch of salt in the food processor. Blend at a low speed, gradually adding the butter until you have a granular structure.

2/ In a separate bowl, mix the egg yolk with the vinegar and 3 tbsp of water, then add the entire mix to the food processor in one go. Add more water if the dough is too crumbly and dry. Wrap the dough in cling film and leave in the refrigerator for at least one hour.

3/ Cut the dough into 6 pieces, roll it out and use it to line the tart moulds. Allow the tart moulds to cool in the refrigerator for another 30 minutes.

4/ Preheat the oven to 350° F. Prick the dough at the base of each tart mould with a fork and bake for 15-18 minutes until light brown. Allow to cool down.

5/ Mix the strawberries with 1 cup of sugar, 2 tbsp of lemon juice and 1/2 cup of water. Allow to sit for 20 minutes. Transfer the liquid to a pan and bring to a boil.

6/ Mix 3 tbsp of corn flour with 2 tbsp of cold water and stir into the boiling liquid until it thickens. Remove pan from heat and allow sauce to cool down completely.

7/ Mix the cold sauce with the strawberries and divide this among the tart moulds, then store in a cool place.

8/ Preheat oven to 400° F. Beat the 5 egg whites with 1 teaspoon of lemon juice until firm. Gradually add 1 cup of sugar until stiff peaks form. Stir the rest of corn flour and divide among the strawberry tarts.

9/ Place the tarts covered with the egg white mix in the oven for 2-3 minutes until the egg white turns brown, then allow to cool down. Serve cold.

Ingredients 6p

1 1/4 cups all-purpose flour, sieved
3 cups sugar
6 tbsp unsalted butter, cubed
1 egg yolk
1/2 tbsp of white wine vinegar
3 cups fresh strawberries, quartered
2 tbsp lemon juice
3 tbsp corn flour
5 egg whites
1/4 tsp salt

Requirements

Food processor
Six tart moulds
(3" diameter), greased
Cling film
Rolling pin

Wine suggestion

Xyris 2009, Giovanni e Francesca Marotti Campi, Marche, Italy

Anna Olson, who rose to fame as a professional chef and pastry chef, has her own TV show, called Fresh, on Food Network Canada, the same network that used to broadcast her Sugar and Kitchen Equipped shows. The author of numerous cookbooks, she has also run several restaurants.

49

Strained Yogurt with Strawberry Consommé and Marinated Rhubarb

Jaymz Pool/Wilde Zwijnen

Preparation

1/ Hang a tea towel above a basin, spoon the yogurt in and let the liquid strain out for 24 hours.

2/ Whip the cream with 1 cup of sugar and the scrapings of 1 vanilla bean, and blend it through the strained yogurt.

3/ Put the strawberries in a stainless steel bowl with 3/4 cup of sugar, tarragon and the gin, cover with cling film and suspend above a pan of gently boiling water for 1 hour.

4/ Mix the rhubarb with the remaining sugar and the vanilla scrapings and let it stand for an hour. In a deep plate, scoop 1 spoonful of strawberries, a generous spoonful of strained yogurt and top with the marinated rhubarb.

Ingredients 4p

4 cups yogurt
2 cups whipping cream
2 cups white caster sugar
Scrapings from the insides
of 2 vanilla beans
2 cups strawberries
1 stem of fresh tarragon,
finely chopped
2 tbsp blackcurrant-flavoured gin
2 stems of rhubarb,
cut into small cubes
Clean tea towel

Wine suggestion

Prosecco, another sparkling wine or a red dessert wine

New Zealand native Jaymz Pool's new restaurant Wilde Zwijnen ('Wild Boars' in English) is located in his own neighbourhood, Amsterdam's so-called 'Indies' district. The vibrant melting pot of cultures in this up-and-coming neighbourhood is reflected in Pool's cooking style.

50

Roasted Bananas with Macadamia Nuts, Honey and Ice Cream

Brian Saword/Don Brioni's Bistro

Preparation

1/ Heat up the barbecue.
Crush the macadamia nuts.
Roast the unpeeled bananas for 5 to 10 minutes on the hot barbecue, turning over halfway through.
Note: the bananas can also be roasted in a very hot oven. Don't roast them too long, but warm them completely through.

2/ Open each banana skin with a fork, spoon some honey and chopped nuts over the bananas then lay them on a plate in a V-shape so that a scoop of ice cream can be put in the middle. Garnish the ice cream with a cherry.

Ideal with a summer barbecue.

Ingredients 4p

8 ripe bananas
4 tbsp honey
4 tbsp macadamia nuts
4 scoops of vanilla ice cream
4 cherries, may be glacé cherries if preferred

Requirements

Barbecue or oven

Wine suggestion

Any sweet wine, such as a Barsac, Stein or Tokay.

Don Brioni's is one of the most famous restaurants in Malawi, and chef Brian Saword has trained a large number of locals in order to give them an opportunity to work in the country's booming restaurant industry.

51

Persian Rose-Saffron Crème with Marinated Figs

Alfons Schuhbeck/Schuhbeck's in den Südtiroler Stuben

Preparation

1/ Preheat oven to 120°F. Remove petals from the roses one by one. Mix 2 tbsp of water with 2 whipped egg whites and use a brush to coat both sides of the petals. Sprinkle the petals on both sides with 3 tbsp of sugar, then place them on a baking tray covered with baking parchment and allow to dry in oven for 3-4 hours. Chop half the petals into rough pieces.

2/ Preheat oven to 355°F. Mix 1 dash of cinnamon with 2 tbsp of sugar and bring to a boil together with the milk, 1 pinch of salt and the content of the vanilla bean. Stir in the dessert rice, add 1 piece of orange peel, cover, and allow to bake in preheated oven for approx. 30 minutes, stirring occasionally.

3/ Heat the orange liqueur, stir in the saffron and allow to sit for 10 minutes.

4/ Dissolve the gelatine in the hot rice. Mix the saffron with the chopped rose petals and the rosewater and allow to cool a little.

Mix the remaining egg whites with the remaining sugar and whisk until creamy. Stir this mixture through the lukewarm rice and allow to cool. Whisk the cream until it has the consistency of yogurt; then lightly beat this mixture through the cooled rice as well.

5/ Place the slices of fig next to each other and sprinkle lightly with icing sugar. Sprinkle the slices with a few drops of lemon juice, then add the remaining cinnamon and a little grated orange peel.

6/ Purée the strawberries together with the sugar and a few drops of lemon juice; then rub through a sieve.

7/ Fill the moulds and allow cream to stiffen in the refrigerator for several hours, keeping moulds covered. Dip the moulds in hot water and drop the puddings into dessert plates. Place the figs next to the moulds and add some drops of strawberry coulis. Sprinkle the remaining rose petals on top.

Ingredients 4p

2 blooming roses, unsprayed
4 egg whites, whipped
1 cup sugar
2 dashes of ground cinnamon
3/4 cup milk
1/2 vanilla bean
1/2 cup dessert rice
2 strips organic lemon peel and orange peel
1 tbsp orange liqueur
1 packet of saffron
2 tsp of gelatine powder
1 tsp rosewater
1/2 cup whipped cream
4 large, ripe figs, peeled and sliced
2 tsp icing sugar
A few drops of lemon juice
1 cup strawberries

Requirements

Four 1 cup moulds
Baking parchment
Hand blender

Wine suggestion

A Riesling Auslese 2003, Markus Molitor Zeltinger Himmelreich, Mosel, Germany.

Chef Alfons Schuhbeck of Munich's Südtiroler Stuben is renowned for his use of regional, seasonal products.

Ginger and Espresso Pear

Yolanda van der Jagt/Daatjes Passie

Preparation

1/ Finely chop the balls of stem ginger and divide half between the four glasses. Peel the pear and cut it into small pieces above the glasses (so as to capture the juice). Spoon a small amount of the ginger syrup from the jar into each glass and divide the remaining chopped ginger on top.

2/ Whip the cream lightly with a whisk so that it is somewhat thicker but still fluid. Spoon the whipped cream onto the ginger in the glasses, sprinkle a little ground espresso on top and serve right away.

3/ It is the blend of flavours and simplicity that makes this dessert so special. If the quantities are halved, it is also suitable as an amuse-bouche between the main course and dessert.

Ingredients 4p

8 balls of stem ginger (from a jar)
2 tbsp ginger syrup
2 ripe Doyenné du Comice pears
4 tbsp whipping cream
1/2 tsp finely ground espresso beans

Requirements

4 glasses

Wine suggestion

A spicy but not-too-sweet dessert wine or a light sparkling wine

After working in a variety of countries for many years, gaining invaluable experience with chefs such as Jamie Oliver, Yolanda van der Jagt returned to the Netherlands to explore her love of traditional Dutch cuisine. She uses local ingredients to create fabulous dishes, a style also embraced by her catering company, Daatjes Passie.

Chef Index

Alfonso Iaccarino/Don Alfonso 1890, Italy/P 35

Alfons Schuhbeck/Schuhbeck's in den Südtiroler Stuben, Germany/P 115

Andreas Caminada/Schloss Schauenstein, Switzerland/P 101

Anna Olson/TV Chef, Canada/P 109

Anne-Sophie Pic/Maison Pic, France/P 81

Anthony Sedlak/TV Chef, Canada/P 75

Bob Blumer/TV Chef, Canada/P 95

Brian Saword/Don Brioni's Bistro, Malawi/P 113

Daniel Boulud/DANIEL, United States/P 57

David Laris/Laris, China/P 89

Davide Oldani/D'O, Italy/P 39

Edwin Kats/InterContinetal, China/P 17

Emmanuel Stroobant/Restaurant Saint Pierre, Singapur/P 47

Erik van Loo/Restaurant Parkheuvel, Netherlands/P 49

Filippo la Mantia/Filippo la Mantia, Italy/P 51

Gennaro Esposito/Torre del Saracino, Italy/P 91

Gert-Jan Cieremans/Seinpost, Netherlands/P 33

Gordon Ramsay/Restaurant Gordon Ramsay, United Kingdom/P 105

Harald Wohlfahrt/Schwarzwaldstube in Hotel Traube Tonbach, Germany/P 83

Heinz Reitbauer/Steirereck Stadtpark, Germany/P 45

Heinz Winkler/Residenz Heinz Winkler, Germany/P 77

Jason Atherton/TV Chef, United Kingdom/P 71

Jaymz Pool/Wilde Zwijnen, Netherlands/P 111

Jean Beddington/Restaurant Beddington's, Netherlands/P 25

Jean Michel Lorain/La Cote Saint Jacques, France/P 73

Jon-Filip Johannessen/Mathuset Solvold, Norway/P 37

Jonnie Boer/De Librije, Netherlands/P 11

Luca Montersino/Golosi di Salute, Italy/P 103

Luke Dale-Roberts/La Colombe, South-Africa/P 15

Magnus Ek/Oaxen Skärgårdskrog, Sweden/P 63

Mauro Colagreco/Mirazur, France/P 27

Michael Caines/Gidleigh Park, United Kingdom/P 107

Michael Smith/Ocean Entertainment, Canada/P 85

Mirko Reeh/Restaurant Pearl by Mirko Reeh, Germany/P 43

Moreno Cedroni/Madonnina del Pescatore, Italy/P 13

Neil Perry/Rockpool, Australia/P 41

Phillipe Rochat/Restaurant de l'Hotel de Ville, Switzerland/P 53

Pierre Gagnaire/Pierre Gagnaire, France/P 19

Ramon Beuk/Ramon Beuk, Netherlands/P 29

Robert Clark/C restaurant, Canada/P 59

Ronald Kunis/Restaurant De Kas, Netherlands/P 79

Rose Reisman/TV Chef, Canada/P 61

Rudolf en Karl Obauer/Obauer, Austria/P 69

Sergio Herman/Oud Sluis, Netherlands/P 31

Stefan Stiller/Stiller's restaurant, China/P 87

Sven Elverfeld/Aqua, Germany/P 23

Tetsuya Wakuda/Tetsuya's restaurant, Australia/P 93

Tim Mälzer/Bullerei, Germany/P 65

Tom Aikens/Tom's Kitchen, United Kingdom/P 67

Victor Arguinzoniz/Asador Etxebarri, Spain/P 21

Yolanda van der Jagt/Daatjes Passie, Netherlands/P 117

Yo Saumande/Auberge Michel, South-Africa/P 99

Colophon, Sponsors, Thank you

Master Chefs for Home Chefs 4 was created though the generosity of several parties (PO Box 30250, 2500 GG The Hague, the Netherlands) in support of the United Nations World Food Programme. This publication was prepared with the utmost care. The parties listed below are not liable for any inaccuracies in the text. For question and comments, please write to the address above.

Recipes edited by Fiona Ivanov, www.beingajellybar.net Translation The Language Lab, www.languagelab.nl Concept & Styling Photography Tyner Mulder @ Special Sauce, www.specialsauce.nl Table decoration Iittala, www.iittala.com Galerie & Winkel Lood om oud glas, www.loodomoudglas.nl / Beeldhouwwinkel Amsterdam, www.beeldhouwwinkel.nl Intercodam, www.intercodam.com / Geke Lensink, www.gekelensink.nl / Studio Bazar, www.studiobazar.nl Food photography Christian Fielden, www.fieldenfotografie.com / Jeroen Egbers @ Special Sauce, www.specialsauce.nl Image editing Rolf de Bakker, www.rolfdim.com Food styling Ruud Siep, www.ruudsiep.nl / Sander de Ponti, www.sanderdeponti.nl / Yvonne Jimmink, yvonne@jimmink.com / John Nijsen, jnijsen@telfort.nl Portraits of children Erik Larkens, Metafoor Media www.metafoormedia.nl / Mariëlle van Spronsen Concept, Design and Layout Bloemendaal in Vorm, Rijssen, www.bloemendaalinvorm.nl Production Boekdrukdeal, www.boekdrukdeal.nl Project Management Canada Luzia Oliveira / Christine Ng/ Julie Marshall Global Project Management Nadine van der Klugt / Carola Edel Mariëlle van Spronsen, info@masterchefsforhomechefs.com

Thank you We would like to thank all 52 Master Chefs for their selfless contribution to this project: we could never have created this wonderful book without you. Thanks also to all the companies that contributed, for showing such willingness to get involved in this project and for supporting this cause by donating their time and talent. Finally we would like to thank all the people and companies that contributed to the book after going to print.

Alexandria Books, www.abebooks.com / Metafoor Media, www.metafoormedia.nl
Bloemendaal in Vorm, www.bloemendaalinvorm.nl
Fotostudio Special Sauce, www.specialsauce.nl / The Language Lab, www.languagelab.nl
TNT, www.tnt.com / Spring Global Mail, www.springglobalmail.com

ISBN: 978-90-79824-07-6

NUR 441

Mixed Sources
Product group from well-managed forests and other controlled sources
www.fsc.org Cert no. SGS-COC-001425
©1996 Forest Stewardship Council
FSC